IGUANAS

WITH...

By Kathleen Connors

Please visit our website, www.garethstevens.com. For a free color catalog of all our high-quality books, call toll free 1-800-542-2595 or fax 1-877-542-2596.

Library of Congress Cataloging-in-Publication Data

Connors, Kathleen.
 Iguanas / Kathleen Connors.
    p. cm. — (Really wild reptiles)
 Includes index.
 ISBN 978-1-4339-8375-7 (pbk.)
 ISBN 978-1-4339-8376-4 (6-pack)
 ISBN 978-1-4339-8374-0 (library binding)
 1. Iguanas—Juvenile literature. I. Title.
 QL666.L25C66 2013
 597.95'42—dc23
                                        2012022906

First Edition

Published in 2013 by
Gareth Stevens Publishing
111 East 14th Street, Suite 349
New York, NY 10003

Copyright © 2013 Gareth Stevens Publishing

Designer: Ben Gardner
Editor: Kristen Rajczak

Photo credits: Cover, p. 1 SuriyaPhoto/Shutterstock.com; p. 5 David Masini/Shutterstock.com; p. 7 Alexander Sviridenkov/Shutterstock.com; p. 9 Joe McDonald/Visuals Unlimited/Getty Images; p. 11 Uradnikov Sergey/Shutterstock.com; p. 13 Brian Lasenby/Shutterstock.com; p. 15 Fabio Lacoponi/Shutterstock.com; p. 17 De Agostini Picture Library/Getty Images; p. 19 Kayla A/Shutterstock.com; p. 21 Irina oxilixo Danilova/Shutterstock.com.

Printed in the United States of America

CPSIA compliance information: Batch #CW13GS: For further information contact Gareth Stevens, New York, New York at 1-800-542-2595.

Contents

Words in the glossary appear in **bold** type the first time they are used in the text.

IS THAT AN IGUANA?

The iguana is one cool-looking lizard! But how do you know if you've seen one? The wildest feature of this amazing **reptile** is how different the many species, or kinds, look from one another. They can range from about 4 inches (10 cm) to almost 7 feet (2.1 m) long!

Iguanas can be many colors, too—from gray to bluish to bright green. In 2009, scientists reported finding pink iguanas! However, very few of these have been found.

What a Wild Life!

There are about 30 species of iguana.

The green iguana is one of the best-known kinds— and it's not always all green!

5

LOOKIN' SHARP

Iguanas are covered in scales and have a row of **spines** down their back. Four short legs end in five toes that look almost like human hands! These toes have sharp claws the iguana uses for climbing.

You can recognize an iguana by the flap of skin under its chin called a dewlap and by the **crest** on top of its head. This lizard also has a long tail. In fact, some iguana's tails are so long that half of the iguana's length is its tail!

crest

spines

tail

dewlap

claws

7

HAPPY HABITATS

Iguana **habitats** are found in Central and South America, Mexico, and in the southwestern United States. They may live as far north as Canada, too. Two kinds of iguana live on the Galapagos Islands, and three species are found in Fiji. The Madagascar iguana lives on the island it's named for, which is off the southeastern coast of Africa.

Depending on the kind of iguana, it may spend more time in trees than on the ground. Some, like the green iguana, make their homes in the rainforest.

The desert iguana likes the dry heat of Nevada, Utah, and Arizona.

What a Wild Life!

There are 11 kinds of iguana that live only on the Caribbean Islands.

9

DON'T CATCH A CHILL!

Most of the time, iguanas look like they're just lying around. Like other reptiles, iguanas are cold-blooded. That means their body temperature depends on their surroundings. Iguanas aren't very active by nature, but their basking, or resting, in the sun keeps them warm.

The temperature can affect an iguana's color. When they're cold, iguanas may become slightly darker in color to take in more heat from the sun. If the temperature is too warm, these lizards might become lighter in color. Wild!

These iguanas are hard at work keeping their temperature steady!

11

LOTS OF GREENS

In the wild, iguanas spend little time looking for food. They're generally herbivores, or plant eaters. Iguanas like to munch on tree leaves, flowers, grass, and fruit. Baby iguanas, and sometimes adults, eat bugs and worms, too.

The **diet** of zoo iguanas might seem pretty wild because they like some of the same foods we do! At the Smithsonian National Zoo in Washington, DC, iguanas eat salads. They love lettuce, carrots, and sweet potatoes.

What a Wild Life!

Young iguanas are brighter colors to blend in with their surroundings. However, they're also small and can be dinner for bigger animals—even other iguanas!

This iguana
has found a
leafy snack!

13

MEETING A MATE

Some of this lazy lizard's wildest **behavior** happens when it's looking for a **mate**. Male iguanas work hard to get a female's attention. They may fight each other, bob their heads around, or do a movement that looks like push-ups!

Some iguanas change color when mating time comes. Both males and females may turn an orange-red color, though males commonly become a brighter orange-red. This can happen all over their body or just on their dewlap, crest, spines, or legs.

What a Wild Life!

Female iguanas choose their mate based on how he looks. They prefer to mate with the largest males.

Iguanas commonly mate in the fall.

15

LITTLE LIZARDS

All iguanas lay eggs. Female iguanas lay their eggs about 2 months after mating. Depending on the species, they may lay as many as 50 eggs at a time! These groups of eggs, called clutches, are buried in nests dug in sandy soils.

After about 2 to 4 months, iguana eggs hatch. Baby iguanas use their little claws to dig out of the nest. They commonly look like little copies of their parents, but they're often more brightly colored.

What a Wild Life!

Only about one-third of iguana eggs produce baby iguanas in the wild. Many are eaten. Others just don't grow properly.

17

FEELING SALTY

Perhaps the wildest-looking species of iguana lives on the Galapagos Islands. The marine iguana has a scary face and spiky scales, but it's harmless. These big iguanas spend most of their time basking in the sun after swimming in the cold Galapagos waters.

Marine iguanas have a weird white "wig." That's because they take in a lot of salt when they eat their favorite food—**algae**. They get rid of extra salt through their noses and it dries into a crust on their heads!

What a Wild Life!

Scientists think the marine iguana may have floated over to the islands from South America millions of years ago.

When marine iguanas get rid of extra salt in their bodes, it's sort of like they're sneezing.

19

KEEPING IGUANAS SAFE

The future of iguanas is in danger. Their habitats are cut down for people to build houses and stores. Animals introduced to areas iguanas live in—such as dogs and rats—may eat iguana eggs and babies. People harm iguana populations by catching them to sell as pets, too.

Zoos are trying to help iguanas by **breeding** them and caring for the babies until they can live in the wild. They want to make sure this awesome reptile is around for a long time!

What a Wild Life!

People in Central and South America eat both adult iguanas and iguana eggs.

Where Do Iguanas Live?

KEY

Iguanas

North America

Europe

Asia

Africa

South America

Madagascar

Austrailia

GLOSSARY

algae: living plantlike things that are mostly found in water

behavior: the way an animal acts

breed: to mate two animals with desired qualities in order to produce more like them

crest: a showy growth on the head of an animal

diet: the food and drink an animal eats

habitat: the natural place where an animal or plant lives

mate: one of two animals that come together to produce babies. Also, to come together to make babies.

reptile: an animal covered with scales or plates that breathes air, has a backbone, and lays eggs, such as a turtle, snake, lizard, or crocodile

spine: one of many stiff, pointed parts growing from an animal

FOR MORE INFORMATION

Books

Hibbert, Clare. *Snakes and Lizards*. Mankato, MN: Arcturus, 2011.

Wojahn, Rebecca Hogue, and Donald Wojahn. *A Rain Forest Food Chain: A Who-Eats-What Adventure in South America*. Minneapolis, MN: Lerner Publications, 2009.

Websites

Green Iguana

animals.nationalgeographic.com/animals/reptiles/green-iguana

Read more about the green iguana and see pictures of it and other reptiles.

Green Iguana Society: Kids Club

greenigsociety.org/kidsclub.htm

Use this website to decide if an iguana is the right pet for you. Play games and take a quiz, too.

Publisher's note to educators and parents: Our editors have carefully reviewed these websites to ensure that they are suitable for students. Many websites change frequently, however, and we cannot guarantee that a site's future contents will continue to meet our high standards of quality and educational value. Be advised that students should be closely supervised whenever they access the Internet.

INDEX